A Walk in the Mindfield / Short Dreams

Kevin J. Mogged

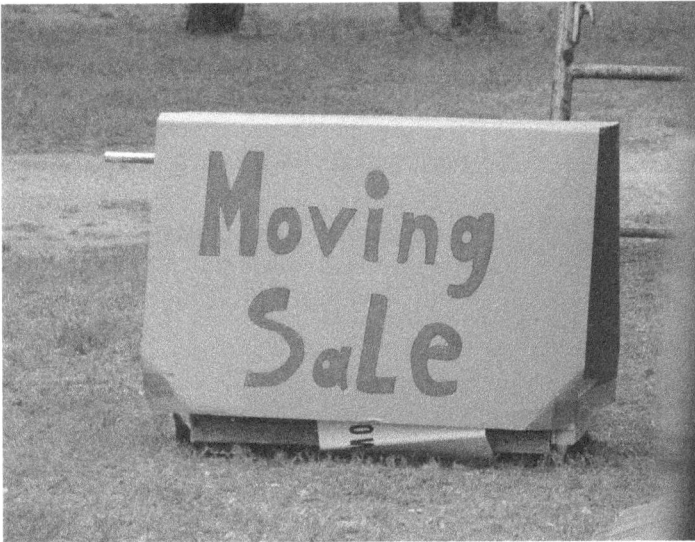

Produced and distributed by
Kevin J. Mogged
PO BOX 312
Krakow, WI 54137

ISBN 978-0-6151-4764-2

Principle Photographer: Kevin J. Mogged

For
nonexistent

Without whom this book would have not existed.

Contents

Foreword

This collection of poetry represents some of the darkest stirrings in the soul. Written during a very radical time of change and unfortunate events. These words should prompt an emotional response. I hope the reader dives into these poems and not only feels the raw emotion, but possibly becomes inspired in some way.

The short story entitled "Short Dreams" is a dark story, but not aimed at the gruesomeness. It was inspired by a Jim Thompson novel named "The Nothing Man". I wanted to capture a more introspective true crime story. Develop the character more through thoughts than actions.

Regardless, enjoy this text in your own way. Just as it was written in my own way.

A Walk in the Mindfield

Wake Up Time

My alarm and time to awaken was 6:00am
This meant that I would wake at 5:00am
Go back to sleep
Then awaken to not only an alarm
Also to my mother's voice
Latent feelings from the past surface
I manage to awaken
I then eat all the pizza

The Curse

Are you cursed?
I am cursed.
I think everyone is cursed.
How do you handle your curse.
Do you slip it away?
Do you sip it away?
Do you handle it gracefully?
Do you throw it in everyone's face?
Is it something you'd like to share?
Will you share it with me?

Dreaming Something

I was dreaming of something
something funny
It made me laugh.
I laughed so hard I woke up
I think I laughed out loud
I was sure someone heard
No one to ask if I laughed
I'm sure they were laughing
At me laughing
Doesn't matter
It was very funny

Pink Shirt

We wait in a room
Much pink about
Two older fellows talking
 about their dying friends
An elegant, but isolated art woman
The foreigners in a foreign country
So much pink
The worst, a boy
I wanted to pop him right in the face
He was so ultimate
With his ultimate woman
Such disgusting things
I should have broken both their noses

write, right?

I could have spent all night typing to you lovelies.
Instead, I had to write for some ungrateful
professor with a PHD.
What could a worm like me offer her.
Besides my left testicle, and a ball of Kleenex.
I would much rather write for the lovelies.
The under-rape-preciated.
The over-worked species.
I could have spent this night creating the
revolution.
I spent it in frustration.
Trying to achieve a mediocre grade for my
mediocre future.
I hope to see you all there.
Very soon.
Plush couches.
Crushed velvet.
Stupid cocktail thingys.
We'll have it all.
We'll even have people controlled by tiny strings
and smooth plastic levers.

! @ wink

The denizen with its dark curled tentacles.
Silent motion unwrapping.
Love not a concept.
Its black leather skin.
Concealing the emotion.
Its evil a natural byproduct of its form.

You too would not want to touch
It consumes fleshy pleasures
A hunter of delicate articles
Stay under the radar
It hunts tonight
Your life
in peril
h
o
l
d
tight

Release

You've released me from your hold.
machine.
You cold piece of metal garbage.
I don't want to touch you.
I've given myself to you.
You've taken years away from me.
No use spitting on you.
I look around and see your payment.
Material.
I remember when I was young.
You were young.
You cradled me against your metal flesh.
You are now a rustic remnant of something that
was great.
I leave you to lay in pieces.
Let the scavengers take what they want.
The rest be buried in the past.
Good Bye machine.

Behind the Back

Whispers and lies
I hope you talk behind my back
The way I talk behind yours
I speak in sensitivity
Trust me
I don't speak in lies
I speak in honesty
I trust you now
I just hope
You trust me
Don't be mad
I don't want to do wrong
I can't let you in
There is no door
You need to trust me
Give me a chance
That's all I can ask for
Talk behind my back
I talk behind yours
That's what friends do

Hearts

Hearts are given
Hearts are taken
Hearts take time
Hearts break
instantly
There is no control
Moved by the hearts whim
Misled
Then pushed aside
Designed to deceive
An instrument of destruction
The ultimate device for
pain

Spitting Cobra

I am the spitting cobra.
I hate what you have given me.
It would give me much pleasure
to sink my fangs in you.
Pierce your red muscle.
Taste your blood firsthand.
I want what is mine
I will have what is mine
I the spitting cobra
Spit on your request.
My love is for the world.
You can't stop me.
I will bring order to this
Then I will spit in your face
Laughing at you

I grow tired of this absurd running
For what?
For what?
I hurt others for being me
I am spitting cobra
Invincible
I am me
Your misunderstanding
Is the weak membrane
inside your skull
Listen to me once
My words ring of logic
These tasks are repetitive
They are no use
I bite and claw at air

It is sad

rw

Everything is so right
It's so wrong
The collapse is in place
I feel it
It's coming
It does
always
I wish for it not
It will happen though
It is the great rebirth
The cycle of time
That isn't the concern
My weakness
is apparent
I expose it to all
Their shadows
surround
I want signs
I want shelter
Comfort
Materials are abundant
time shortens
feelings
immortal

Silver Web

The insects twitching.
Hundreds
My spider workers
Spread thin
Come back, come back
You little shits
You listen to me
I made this silver web for you
Why you treat your master this way
I give you the path
I feed you, you do what I say.
Look at me with your multi-faceted eyes when I
speak to you
Why confuse me
We could be so much more
focused

press

Force
Pressure
Breathe
Pointless effort
Locked and strangled
Need to get a grip
See an end
I can't
I stay
Lost and tense
Fresh air
Secluded in it
I can stop anytime
A little water
Breathe
Can't
Someone is pushing
down
I can't get up
I sometimes walk around
Aimless and defenseless
Mindless and senseless
It was all clear
one day
Now it's clouded
No direction or luck
Maybe a bag of chips
That could release it's hold
I just want
something
I don't know

particles

I see fragments
Like always
I see remnants
Something I love
The trails
I don't understand
I feel
I don't understand
It all fits
Somehow
It all fits
I don't fit
There was a time
When everything made sense
It all fit
I fit
somehow
Now
I don't fit
I think I don't fit
Pieces in front
I try to place
Afraid of how they fit
Want something
How do they fit
Wish to bring close
The pieces
they push
Why
Why is it
Why is I

Strong
Weak
Strong
Weak
The tale
Is it near the end?
How does it cope?
It's knowledge a burden.
It wants out.
It wants in.
It's forcing it's face.
The surface.
Where false things lie.
Submerge.
In depths of safety.
senseless
someone knows

quota

I've hit my quota
I will be
punished
severely
In the utmost of tolerance
Pain
will rain down
on the pieces
My fear
is concealed
I have no wrong
This race
is wrong
I feel blood
More blood
is good
The time
has come
The test
is near
Let evil
approach
I fear
nothing
For
there is
nothing

Little Thoughts

lighters
little drips
drops
time in stasis
elements of adoration
triangles
not in style
bring light in
cast dark out
draw on the wind
careful canvas
direct poles
helpless carrier
nickels
dimes
liquid lizards
hunt freedom
disintegrate
never
nothing

Mogged

I am Mogged
If you can't handle that step away.
I'll eat your fucking soul.
I hate you
I give you life
What you want I have
I have to let you have it
you have to work at it
I don't like you
but I'll be your friend
I'll give you life
If you want to work for it
I'm not your friend.
I'm your worst enemy, but you need to be that
I'll suck your soul
You need it
You need to refresh your being
you are weak
I am strong
I feed off you
you learn from me
I make you strong.
Come with me
dance the dance
if you keep up
we will be
if not.
you will be
I like you the way you are
you are weak
I am strong

you come with me
you keep up
you be strong like me
I keep you
you like you
me I'll be me
we are strong
you'll see

U Turn

You wonder why I want to leave
Fucking bullshit snow
This state won't let me go
It employs me
It feeds me
It befriends me
It shelters me
Then it beats and destroys me
What I would give for the release
The pain this place gives
It knows how to grind
I feel no warmth
I feel no path of retreat
I am sold and retired
My spirit asleep
Haunted
Hurt
Diluted

Excited

I get up
I'm excited
I walk over here
I'm excited
Why can't I stop
I'm excited
Something new
I'm excited
Stop it now
I'm excited
Please, stop
I'm excited
No, don't do that
I'm excited
Go to sleep
I"m excited
I wish it would just stop
I'm excited
I don't care, I just want to calm
I'm excited
Does anyone realize
I'm excited
Is there some kind of repair
I'm excited
It must end
I'm excited
unbearable

Crust

Specks of mud
Encrusting
Despair
Dying
Liver
Onions
Disgusting
These things are

Envelope

I've been placed thru an envelope
Delivered to everyone
I know what you all want
I think I want it too
I'm in all your heads
I make you want it too
I'm your sun
your rain
your dirt
Can you feel the grit?
Grinding in your teeth
That is me
I haven't gotten to that soul
I will
They will feel the deep sensation
The grime in their hair
I want to impart something spectacular
Something ill
That feeling
In your stomach
It's me
Floating and flopping
I make you sick
You can breathe it
I make you
Your plans
are all my plans
I set the motion
You can't help
You float along
It is too vast

You feel what you feel
I make it so

Mindscapes

The mind is my final escape.
It is my one sanctuary.
It is my biggest enemy.
It is my best friend.
Where I can hide.
Where I can play.
Where I can decide.
Do they even know what's going on inside here?
What do they say when I'm not near?
Do they dare say a thing?
Do they hide it in their minds?
Cursed them.
They can hide it in theirs, but I won't let them in mine.

Enemies

Anger and fear are your enemies
I am not
Conflict is for the weak
I seek resolution
Not vengeance
Time is limited
You still have time
There is always time
Sometimes winning is taking defeat
The strong will remain with their head high
Strength lies in three
One of the three collapses
The other two will fall
When judgment falls
Don't have collected guilt in your heart

Commonality

I was not installed with the common interface
I speak in proxy
I only appear to be compatible with human version
20.0.7
I speak in emulation
I watch them
They move and talk synergistic
I move and talk independent of the design
They have their parties
gatherings
I only appear in ghost
Sometimes they notice
Sometimes I choose their notice
I keep my insides, inside
That is where I like to hide
They are speaking and moving
I only appear to speak and move
My deceptive form emerges
They think they know my form
It is a trick
It is a proxy
A proxy by desire

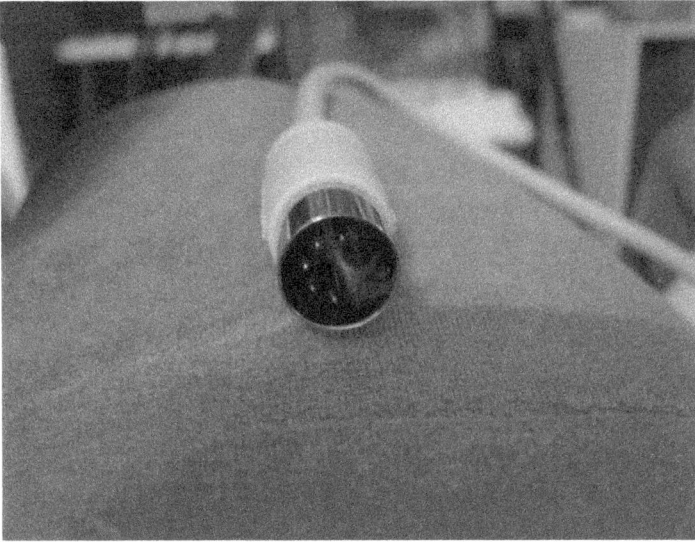

Simple

Simple Minds
chasing a single focal point
Billions of stars
Regretfully, they chase a single sun
I wish you could be me
I wish I could be more
Push your curiosity further
Didn't you want more?
I wanted more
It drove me here
I keep asking for more
Sometimes I feel the edge
I then ask for more
It sometimes comes
It sometimes loops
There was a time
There is a time
There will be a time
A continuous loop
I search for the epicenter
I think I know where it is
Do I dare travel it?
Does anyone dare travel it with me?
It will be an end, and a beginning
It will kill and renew
How I wish I could be you
It's too late
The box has been opened
My life is in limbo
How I'd like to share
It can't be understood

Stumble

Stumble
Stumble
Trip
Fall
Why can't I make sense of it all?
Will I lift the right stone?
Friends
Family
They seem to fade
It's just me
and the demons
they live inside of me
I have had dreams
Some of those dreams are gone
Some have stayed
Are dreams real?
I've been told to have goals
They aren't my goals
Some people live their dreams
Some fail
Some live the lie
I don't want the lie
I am a wild animal
I am designed to survive
I will live
Live in uncertainty
There has never been a course laid out

As I Sit

As I sit, I think of all the biological processes
happening.
The invisible and the visible.
I think of how my personality shifts back and forth.
Time is not real, but change is.
Why does something appeal one day and never
the same after?
Why do somethings grow into something bigger
yet remain the same?
How can something remain the same no matter
how worn out it is?
How can that thing bring the senses straight into
the past?
These are just a few of the things I think of as I sit.

Follow

We know what we are taught.
We aren't taught by ourselves.
The mistake of others.
Not taught as hunters.
Followers to our guides.
Not realizing the latent abilities.
Have we been taught by our mirror.
We would have seeked long ago.
The reward fit for the king.

Until we detach from our mentors.
We have not found.
The knowledge we have.
We didn't realize was around.

The true teacher revealed.
Is waiting in the student.

The best mentor will show.
Show the true teacher.
Show the way home.

Thousand

A thousand thoughts
A hundred concerns
A dozen broken parts
Transparent organs
Pumping black fluids
Optic device probing
Searching, waiting, hoping
Thinking, turning
Into a hungry instrument
Designed to inflict pain
Designed to feel pain
Stalking the land
Colors, sound
Recording importance
Disposing hatred, uncleanliness
Instigator
Destroyer
Life giver
Bleed
Cough Sneeze
Please
Smashing existence
Polling love
Small
insignificant values
Gyros cutting flesh
Melting the slices together
In special tasteless mass
Made to amaze
Made to love

The Price

How much is your life worth?
How much is my life worth?
How much is their life worth?
Is their life worth less than the money in your
hand?
Is your life worth more than the money in your
hand?
How can you speak the way you speak.
They want you dead.
Did you realize that?
You feel uncomfortable in your chair?
You wanted them dead.
Didn't you?
I can't change your mind.
You'll never change.
A filthy greedy monster I abhor.
You deserve the wrath you inflict.
Just you don't realize what you have done.

Cry

What does it feel like to cry?
What makes water drip from your eyes?
Is there something missing?
Are you broken?
Can you be fixed?
Is it permanent?
Where do you turn it off?
I know why I cry.
I have reason to.
I try opening the ducts wide.
Nothing exits.
The water is dried up.
There is a draught of emotion.
For reasons unknown.
Some reasons known.
Can't be so simple.
is there something missing?
Am I broken?
Can I be fixed?
is it permanent?
Where do I turn it on?

Seam

Stepping through time.
Walking in folds.
Peering into membrane.
The otherside.
Clear world.
Inside vast.
Inside hollow.
Mud.
Shifting hallways.
Feeding gray colors.
Outside the sun.
Inside pain.
The 2 worlds.
What is shared.
What is seen.
What is invisible.
What is in between.

Opening Up

The world is opening up.
It's exciting.
Doesn't make sense.
Makes no sense.
Why is this happening today?
These days?
Will it continue?
It may fade in a splash of certainty and boredom.
Don't need to know.
Just need to ride out the wave.
Hope the wave continues.
Hope it doesn't fizzle out.
Hope that everything will make sense.
Hope that it continues to remain a mystery.
Can't move back.
Should move forward.
Stay clear.
Stay confident.
Don't let them know what is going on.
Just continue on the path.
As if it happened.
The way they think.
They will never know.
Until it's too late.
Then they will know the greatness.
They will know something that will no longer be
important.
It will just be.
Continue to look for the openings.
Let the world open up.
Swallow the feelings.

Swallow the sorrow.
Make it all new once again.

Days Become Years

Days become years.
People become memories.
Where did the boy go?
The one I used to know.
Who is this boy?
The dull know-it-all.
Is he lost too?
Has he lost his way?
With the rise of mediocrity.
There is a loss of a soul.
The boy is tainted.
The boy is lost.
Will he be waiting at the station?

Idiot

Make me feel like an idiot.
I am no fool.
I just want to be cool with you.
Why am I dizzy with my mind.
I am usually quite kind.
I now don't use the right tools.
I am simple with a needle and a spool.
I look at life and it makes no sense.
I don't see why people can't be happy and dance.
In my childhood I knew of a place.
Where cares dissolved.
People embraced.
Talk of silly things.
Where this place has gone.
I don't know.
I'd love to take you there if I knew how.
My plane is broke I can't fly now.
Maybe I need help, somehow.
A way to laugh.
A way to not frown.
A way that will save me from being down.
I want to help you.
I want to help me.
There has to be some way to be.

Mind, the Marriage

Day starts.
Day stops.
The chunk of matter stays.
Take it away.
Give me a new one.
This one is used.
It is soiled.
It talks nonsensically.
The solder has lifted.
The solution is not tasteful.

The spiral begins.
It worsens.
It continues down its path.
Winding weaker and weaker.
Till the end is apparent.
The solution is reached.
The bindings are released.

Logic is the ultimate answer.
You have been let a stray.
Your logic has broken.
You can't be saved now.

Emotion gives pleasure.
Emotion gives pain.
It smears the mind.
Makes you a fool.

I was human once.
I had a heart.

I had a soul.
Am I just flesh?
Did I loose the things dear to me?

The past is an indelible mark.
Move past something that can't be removed?
It remains.
It's never forgotten.
A reminder.
Reminder of how human we are.
How human I once was.

My cables feel twisted around me.
I can't break free.
Am I to live this cursed existence?
Is that the destiny set.
Is destiny available to mankind.

How to fit through the holes in the sieve.
There must be a safe place on the other side.
This side is dangerous.
Everything is hurt that I touch.
I am a danger.
Reprogramming of the coil is necessity.
Escaping the coil is impossible.
Reversing the coil is impossible.

Things of haste.
Things of regret.

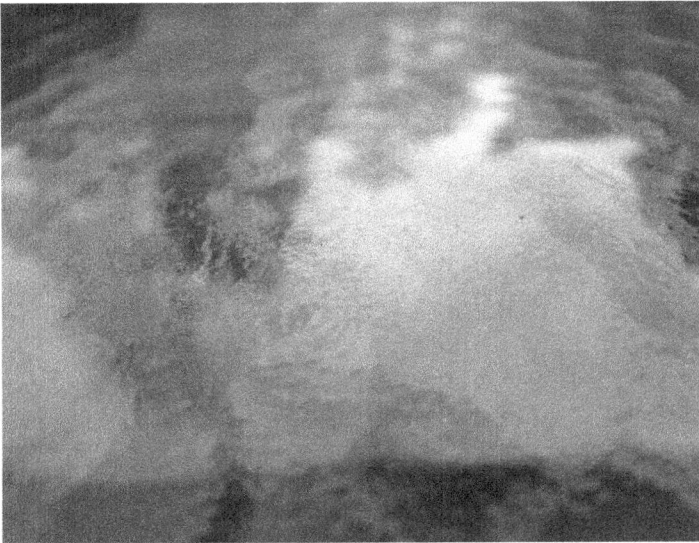

Lost

I went out on a journey alone.
Staying at home, but leaving that home.
I thought I could do that.
It doesn't seem so.
The home is a solid enclosure.
Tombs have been more inviting.
I wander in search of scraps from the living.
Their lives seem so colorful.
So fake.
I have the luxury of loneliness.
Time mocking me at my side.
Fingers of happiness touch my shoulder.
They tap out a rhythm and play their games.
I don't know their games.
The beginning and the end are sisters.
Sometimes I can't tell them apart.
One leading to the other.
Never in parts.
I lost the way.
I'm not sure if I'll be home for supper.
It's getting late and I have no way.
Please help me, I'm a stray.

Favorite Things

Biting
Clawing
Scraping
Crawling
These are a few of my favorite things

Falling
Twisting
Turning
Learning
Yearn for a direction

Hungry people walking the streets
Step back and watch
Makes them simple
Step forward and the hunt is on
Become blinded in complexities of a cloud
The simple things become the complex act
Are you in or are you out?
They will see you in the spot light.
I will see you in the spot light.

Bastards

You are all bastards
just as I am a bastard
I love you all
I hope you are happy loving me
I'll love you like the evil bastard I am
I hope your vomit stains the world
Leave the mark of hate upon the steps of
mightiness

Working on the Universe

There is no good and bad.
There is yes, no.
positive, negative.
black, white.
balance does not have moral grounds.
It is not justice.
There is balance and being out of balance.
Balance is good.
Being out of balance is temporarily bad.
Till placed back into balance.
Some actions can give a larger modifier.
Sometimes smaller actions are required to fill that larger action.
Sometimes a large force can solve many small built up actions.
The means maybe mysterious or misunderstood.
It is best done in a subtle pro-active movement.
Sometimes a push to unbalance a situation may cause some excitement.
That excitement can be used to fuel a push in the opposite direction towards balance.
This may cause new linkages.
I most go work in the other realm.
Don't fret.
I will return soon.

Fix IT

Fixing computers involves a lot of waiting.
It's not as exciting as on tv.
It's wait, wait, walT.
A lot of times you are working on machines that
shouldn't even be running Winblows.
That's because people are cheap.
People don't care about quality anymore.
They just want cheap.
now I'm in class doing the walTing.
I get to go back to work and do more walTing.
A lot of people can't put up with my walTing.
They get mad.
Do they think I like the walTing.
I'm good at the profession of walTing.
That's why I have a laptop.
I can then write things like this.
While walTing.

Instant Death

Grasping the collar pulling the chain.
Push, pull, push away.
In the black of night the train travels into the day.
It's big iron heart edging into the horizon.
This is the new dawn.
The snail creeping across the lawn.
It's simple brain projecting the terrain.
It doesn't remember where it's gone, and not
where it yet shall become.
It's voyage not long, but important all the same.
Would I want known future? No!
That is instant death.

Mind Blender

The moments before sleep.
Desperation in thought.
Moments left.
Nearing end.
lights out.
Chaos within.
Chaos creates questions.
Chaos draws answers.
Awake.
Chaos frightens.
Asleep.
Chaos wains.
Awake.
The day has come.
The heroes are gone.
Must stay occupied.
Asleep.
Awake.
Damn.
Lost time.
continue.
Asleep.
darkness.
Awake.
Damn.
Who was that.
Let's go.
Asleep.
Awake.
continue.
continue.

Sketches

In my sketchbook of desire.
I draw the things I want.
They can't be seen.
They are sometimes feelings.
Sometimes obscene.
They come alive in color.
So perfect and clean.
Can one day they become a feeling.
A feeling to hold.
Inside.
This is not what I was told.
You must do this.
You must find that.
That is not right.
This is what is correct.
Sometimes I'm not sure what or who to believe.
Maybe this all.
Was just a dream.

Fragments

As I walk through the forest of dreams I notice fragments of me. Pieces of my past, present, and possible future. The fragments are more elaborate than that. This is no simple Dickens tale, this is what is laid in front of the mind. There is no possible way to layout the tangled branches of the mind. We all walk that path alone until the path no longer remains. Some of the fragments contain other fragments that exist in other areas equally as well. These fragments aren't the simple memories, but data foretelling the future and explaining the past. Some too late, some too soon. I question if they could be assembled and formed to create something new. Seems the new forms are just what they were. A change, but only a shift from the original forms. They are changed in a way that is completely the same. Should the fragments be changed? To curious not to change them. There seems to be no way of removal. They are indelible marks. Is there a way to unlock the mysteries of these puzzles? I can't tell you, that is the quest I take. To define the undefinable. Find a solution to a puzzle plaguing the mind. The puzzle quite possibly being the mind. They haunt to the very soul.

Lectric Love Like Me

Screeching Bonneviles
I supply
A song
I no longer can place
About love
True love
Foreverness
The governess of the soul
A joke
Really
Something misplaced
The cosmos not giveth
My dreams
Unknown
I know
You don't
You don't feel
You don't place them
Short term
Destruction
What is important
A shelter
Food
Water
What of the soul
The soul yearns
for
love
art
meaning
Where are the tears

The feelings
What is this?
Not over
yet
Safe one day
one day more
Simple
It is
It really
is
I love simplicity
I am simple
A circuit
Designed for reception
What happened
sadness folds

Dear Mr. Jaeger

Oh the harshness of the bottle
 then the sweet release of the chaser.
Sometimes it's much easier then this.
If I were brilliant I would mix down the burn.
Under the influence this doesn't always make
sense.
Today, I wanted to visit an old friend
 Mr. Jaeger
He is a good pal.
I met his distant cousin Alpine Wolfe around New
Years.
He was not to kind.
Although, a full bottle will do that to you.
I'm not sure what happened.
Mr. Jaeger was not too kind to me this night.
I'm not sure where we went wrong.
I'll try again soon.
Maybe with a chaser.
Maybe with a little boost.
When I try to drink.
It doesn't work.
When I just drink.
It's just natural.

Her Love

I sit down
She is busy
She eyes me I'm sure
She most likely wants me
The way she pretends
Pretends to be occupied
She is watching my every move
I don't even know what she looks like
I'm sure she's young
Impatient
She wants to speak
 so badly
She enters the plane
I try not to view
She wants that
She's looking for that
What she wants can never be
I'm a loner
I will never be loved
I will never be understood
I'm one of a kind
My kind lives alone
Without the pleasures of love
Just sick
Lost on the plane
We disembark
She hugs her waiting love

Faery Tales

Young Children
Told faery tales
Monster stories
 for behavior
Children grow
Wish of the faery tale
Find the monster
Who is the hero
Didn't realize
 the monster
 is truth
The monster is
 them

Ordinary

I woke up today thinking that it would be an
ordinary day,
and it was.

ladder

The rungs of the ladder are empty.
Should we climb the rungs of the ladder?
What forbidden pleasures await at the top?
What if we shall fall?
Who will stay behind and catch us if we fall?

I know too well the dangers of the ladder.
I have fallen before.
I don't want to fall again.
Give up now.
Never find what I seek.

What do I seek?
Mortal pleasures?
Immortality?
Divine knowledge?
Destroy the ladder?

Life is about calculated risks.
We miss some.
We take others.
Never knowing the life we have disposed of.

pain

Climbing out of a black hole
Hear the world move by
There is no place for me here
I contemplate my sanity
I contemplate your sanity
I am a sleeping tool of destruction
Ready to spring forth and bring justification
My discipline broken
Angered by dark events
Soul on loan and borrowed

I hear the world move by
Where is it moving to?
It came from the same origin
It will end at this origin
Should the unjust pay?
These hours of isolation
Do they make any sense?
What is the accumulated result?

I do hear the world move by
The dust builds
Time can be seen in the sink
The world is lit by dead
You come to me in my sleep
The small periods of time

I am hearing the world go by
I am sitting
I am waiting

panic

Unknown force.
A breaking force.
Disrupting the flow.
A crushing blow.
No bones broken.
No skin punctured.
The mind left vulnerable.

Warfare waged.
Mental struggles.
Unmerited fears.
Self defeating cognition.

Must run.
Must get down and hide.
There is no escape.
No escape from the things in your head.
Wish it was written off as a dream.
It will remain as a reminder.
A reminder of the madness.

Confront something sourced from the inside.
Something controlled.
Something that went out of control.
Need assistance.
Something no one can fix.
A stray thought.
Let it go.
Surgically remove?
It will never leave.
It lives on.

Cage

You keep me locked up.
Poke me with your hot stick.
In my eyes.
Set me free!
Set me out of this cage.
What do you want from me.
I've given you all I can.
You continue to shackle my heart.
My mind runs wild.
The body wishes to follow.
It is left beaten behind.

I am not a flame to be tamed.
I am a wildfire, waiting to break loose.
Spread fury on the land.

You've had your fun.
You're not the only one.
Who wants pleasure.

Let the beast loose.
Let the village crumble.
Empires shake.

Feel what's inside.
Do the right thing.
Turn the key.
Sign the paper.
Push the switch.

Inside the cage.

I pace.
It's alright.
I'll bide my time here.
Someday my rage.
It will show its wonderful power.
The tape will be peeled.
Like the thin coating of skin.
On the frail.

Let's Take a Walk

In a poof of illogic, God does exist.
God hates you.
The same way I hate you.
You are inferior.
Meaningless and dumb.
Pointless creations.
Patrolling a small vector of worthlessness.
I just want to take a walk.
Creating elaborate and laborious reasons.
We are a stupid race.
Wasting wisdom and time on questions.
Questions that have been answered.
Fearful of destruction.
I just want to take a walk.
Connect in a simple fashion.
Take a simple feeling.
Embrace that tiny pleasure.
A pleasure of something small.
Something meaningless, but connected.
Connected in a simple and intricate manner.
Something unexplained.
Something carnal.
We are engulfed by the complicated.
Give no time to our animalistic pleasures.
The core to our beings.
A whole world awaits.
Wasted effort on a world that will crumble.
There is a world at the finger tips.
It just needs to be tapped.
I just want to take a walk.
Emotions are trapped.

Their freedom hindered by fear.
Fears of past reflections.
True happiness is an illusion.
There is only pain.
There is only pleasure.

way of life

Start
Start
Start
The recording never completes
Adds to the mix
Give into routine?
Run from artistry?
One Thing
What a bore
I have unlimited possibilities
There is no end though
No single route
Ideas
Ideas
Ideas
Only place I can put them on
Is this electronic pad of paper
What use is this chronicle?
I won't read it in one hour
Will I read it in a year?
Perhaps

Smoke makes me sick
I'm tired and bored
Don't want to be awake.
I'd like to be home, but it's way too late
I've fallen into a sad state
All I have is this to give to you
My last movements of awake

That Love Time of Year Again

Your blood is red and so is mine.
Why don't we smear it all of the time
You look at me.
I'll spit on you.
Now you eat my toenail stew.
You always lie
That's why I love you so
When I die
I'll never let you go

Caged Animals

We are vicious animals.
Caged by our own minds.
Both spewing love and hate.
Making sense.
Making nonsense.
It's meshed.
It's harmonized.
There is no flesh.
Traveling the synapse.
From one neuron to the next neuron.
Where do they travel?
A struggle in silence brews.
The fall of man has no effect on the fall of one
man.
The brash behavior of one equalling none.
There are paths and steps to take.
There may not be enough time.
Enough time for reason to become reality.
Your cushion is a temporary feeling.
Our lack of cushion pushes the destruction
forward.
Destruction of paths paved by eons.
These paths will be washed with new cleanliness.
Tears may fall.
Tears may dry up.
Only thing left is perception of time in motion.

emptiness

Emptiness
Common word to us
The few or many
I feel it
Feel it in the many pieces
Places that the light shines through
Holes in the windows
Holes in the bricks
What does it take to fill
To fill those spaces
The spaces emptied
Late in the night
In the night I put my fingers through
I feel that coldness travel
What must I do
What must I say
Where must I go
Make things feel not so gray
Tears have dried up long ago
Disgust pushes the levers
Disgust pushes
Emptiness returns
Pushes disgust away
Then envelopes existence

The Wind

Where have the lights gone?
Did they die?
Did something break them?
Where did they go?
How do I get them back?
Why won't they shine?
All is black.
So many.
Now so few.
How do I resurrect the dead?
Will they return on their own ability?
Time goes by so quickly.
It isn't realized till the end.
The end comes quick.
When it does.
The end is the end.
Too late, too bad.

The Beloved

Oh, she lies next to me.
How lovely is she.
If only she'd stay for eternity.
I'm locked in her silhouette.
Her form is so fragile.
Do I even dare touch.
Afraid she may crumble.
She is asleep.
I am not able to wake.
Her hair so perfect and neat.
I could lay beside her forever.
Her radiance touches every part of me.

Who knocks at my door?
Who disturbs the perfection of this moment?
The beauty destroyed instantly.

"This is the police, open up!"
"We know what you have done!"

Split Apart

Peeled and unwrapped
Spread open for all to see
They look inside me

My brain dismantled
The heart stepped on the floor
Intestines squeezed in clinched fists

Scream with no sound
Gesture with no movement

The pain become distant echoes
Sight starts blurring

It's over
peace

Shock and burning
The pieces are put back in
Anger and betrayal

What did they do with the mind?
Who's thoughts are these?
Give it back

Pushed into the street
Alone
Deserted

They'll come looking
They'll come to change it again

They always do

That's what they do
They won't leave me alone
I'm abandoned shortly

These new thoughts are mine
They'll come and rip them out again
Put someone else's thoughts in the shell

They are always watching
Always delivering
I will always be haunted

indecision

Shadows surround and look down.

They don't move or speak.
I think they move.
I think they speak.
I think they speak of what I am.

What am I?
What should I be?
What will I be?

Are they laughing at me?
Are they mocking me?

Why can't I hear them speak?
Why can't I see them move?

I need to know what I did.
I need to know what I was doing.

I know they saw it.
What did they see?

I carefully wrap the ideas.
They see it all.
They see the dirty truth.

Why can't I see them move?
Why can't I hear them talk?

Is this the end of me?

Where does the beginning start?

I need to ask them to ask me.
Then I can find out.
Then I can find the answer to my question.

I am in the middle of a sale.
I need to know the price.
I need to know what is for sale.
It won't matter anyway.
It's not worth the time.

If there is something left.
I think I found it.
I will never find it.
The thing that is left.

Here is the end.
I thought it was the beginning.
I was wrong.
It is the beginning.

eternity

Humanity wants something that won't go away
Something that won't rot or decay
Something that will just stay

Dreams and locations are invented
A god who always forgives you
A place for the dead
True love
Invincible heroes

Construct things that seem indestructible
Statues
Plaques
Buildings

Our real heroes pass away
Loves fades away
We grow older ever day

We trick ourselves in forgetting
This lie fills us with artificial hope

We strive to leave something awesome behind
We fail to realize everything fades
It fades fast
It fades slow
It will fade away

Institutions are built to slow down the fade
We don't want the future to forget the past
All our hard work

A select few decides what fades

The animals choose to fade with no trace
They are simple components to the system

Humans choose to leave large traces
We find it important to scar the world
We want to think we were important in this
machine
Even though we are all just components
Replaceable
Recyclable

Why does mankind not enjoy the temporary and
randomness of the fade
Clean is ugly

The cracks
The lines
The rot
Is unique

The faults
Is beauty

Perfection is different

Short Dreams

I won't lie to you.
Not this time at least.
Where I go is my business. It is my way.
I've been sitting in a dark, empty room for too long.
I know I'm mainly talking to myself, but I like to
think someone is listening.
The bars at night are empty shameful things.
I sit down at the inviting stool and ask for a
whiskey on the rocks.
It's what I do.
After I satisfy my need to hold something cold and
wet
I look at my surroundings.
I see a deserted booth.
Could have had the most wonderful conversation
at one time.
Now it's a wreck.
Not much interest.
A man, wrinkled, packs his cigarette.
He lights it, blocking the wind that is not kissing
the flame.
An over excited girl who isn't impressing with her
mind.
She wanders, looking for the next possible
romantic.
Overlooking my straightforward approach of life.
An overweight lady who could treat a man right if
she could treat herself right.
Her personality struggles through the large flesh.
It's a pity.
Countless kids crowding a pool table.
Their lives focused on a Summer that will run past.
They will not realize this is the best Summer of
their life.

Then.
It was her.
She was quiet.
Sophisticated, and well kept.
She had been through hell.
You wouldn't know it though.
Her movements were deliberate.
They were controlled by an organized team.
Her ability immense.
She was not sure of herself, but she was sure of
the facts.
Sure of what she wanted.
Not sure of the how, what, why.
She knew the when and it was now.
My approach is not-existent.
She approached me.
She was unsure.
She had a simple probe.
"What you drinking?"
This could not be idle chit chat.
She wanted it all.
The entire collection.
How could I answer such an intense question?
"Whiskey.....on the rocks, what would you like?"
I'm sure her mind reeled at a statement like that.
That was way farther than the simple reply that
should have appeared in her mind.
"I would like a vodka martini, dirty. Hold the olives"
At this point. The mind is muddled.
There couldn't be anything so perfect.
It was completely wrong.
After trading pleasantries I left with her in tow.
She is a perfect thing.
Perfect as madness is the most amazing human

behavior.
Her certainty of people and her uncertainty of
herself made a concoction that made anything
other than... a simple cutout, complacent, ordinary.
We drove very fast.
I should say I drove very fast.
Not to reach the destination in shorter time.
I never worry of time.
I like the danger.
Time stands still in the presence of danger.
She was dangerous.
A marvelous machine of danger.
She was ready to show me her danger.
She would show me this danger in her terms.
We entered the beach.
You never hear of people entering the beach.
That's why we did.
It didn't matter what we said.
We said things that didn't make sense.
The talking was just to attach to the feelings
floating through the space.
These feelings some would call love.
I'm not sure what I would call them.
They were short in time, but long in heart.
She cried out loud as I pierced her heart.
I brought the knife hard through the perfect flesh.
Even as the warm red spattered her chest
she was perfect in every way.
She was at the peak of her being.
I wanted to feel that.
To keep that never changing.
It ended.
Her mechanics stopped.
Lifeless would not do it justice.

Unless you felt that word.
Her magic flowed out of her body.
Her brilliance dimmed.
 I felt robbed.
Robbed that I couldn't keep that.
I wanted her.
Even stranger.
She wanted me.
She could have changed me if she wanted.
For the better.
I could have changed her.
I did.
I did for the worse.
I wanted her sealed in plastic.
Even plastic could not keep her.
It was done.
I may have screwed up.
I hate to think that.
I like to think optimistic.
This was meant to be.
I may have saved myself some agony.
I will now be alone.
Like before.
Safe in a cocoon of pity.
Everyone will feel sorrow.
I will do my civic duty, announce that I'm proud
and glad.
I must clean this up.
I must make things back to normal.
I did that.
I won't tell you how.
You have to learn yourself.
My techniques are mine.
I'm not proud.

I went home.
Cleaned myself up.
A warm shower always puts me on track.
I headed to the kitchen.
The ice dispenser decided not to make ice for me.
I'll fix that someday.
I took a glass and filled it with a nice bourbon.
I don't have much, but booze is one thing I keep in supply.
It's based off my demand.
Taking a swig of that cooled me down.
I could then sit at my desk.
A gnarled desk which I found at the side of the road.
You can live so simple if you choose.
It allows you to think of the important things.
That girl was something.
I will now sleep, since I am beat.
Wiping the crust from my eyes. I awaken with interest towards the news.
There is no news of the murder.
I feel as if it didn't happen.
I remember it clear enough.
She was such a perfect thing with that ember glowing bright.
I could have taken her anywhere.
Now she's gone.
Probably better that way.
She was only kidding herself.
I'll see her when I get to hell.
That makes me laugh.
I'm going to have a drink and some fried eggs.
That will make me feel better over everything.
This day seems like a waste.

I think I'll work on what I do best.
Nothing.
Listening to Autechre makes me realize that
simplicity and complexity is the same thing.
I maybe talking out of my ass, but...
I'm not talking about how a complex thing is built
on many simple things.
As a complex idea or item is developed it
becomes a simple idea or item.
Your complex idea is a muddy thought.
As you work it out.
The item becomes clearer and clearer.
You develop it and it takes form.
It then becomes a tangent creation.
It then becomes marketable and mass-produced.
The complex item has become a household word.
Maybe tomorrow will be interesting.
The news actually mentions the body.
Life becomes exciting.
I wanted to hold her.
She didn't look as pure.
Pale and limp.
Two words.
Only one word possibly being attractive.
The other word not typically associated.
A can of ham and beans.
I then sleep.
I walk to the market on occasion.
I dread it.
They look at me.
I stare back sometimes.
They then look upset.
I wasn't looking at them.
I was mirroring their eyes.

A couple cans of beans, some eggs.
I'll have some beef jerky.
That's a real treat.
Stuff never goes bad.
Keep it handy.
In case things get too out of hand.
Those lights so foreign.
I know them though.
"Good day officer, how are you?"
"You are coming with us."
"What is the problem?"
"We have some questions."
How rude, me with food and all.
Something I'm sure will happen.
I'll loose all my food.
I won't be happy.
They are questioning me. It's very hard.
These questions.
They want me to break.
I went out. Spent sometime with a girl.
What is the big deal.
Her death really wasn't a big deal.
In fact.
I think I dreamt it up.
To find someone so perfect.
That is a once in a lifetime.
I wouldn't have killed her.
I have no one.
No one will ever talk to me.
I told them how I felt.
They let me go.
They admitted they had nothing.
The barkeep wasn't sure if we left together.
I don't think we did.

I left by myself.
I went home and fixed a small drink.
Partly through that drink
I decided there was no point and that I should sleep.
Dumping the rest I retired and that was that.
I didn't take a girl with me.
I didn't enter the beach.
I went home.
Alone.
Miserable as usual.
Sulking to the invisible crowd.
There was no perfect vision.
There was me and the whirlwind of my mind.
How dare they question me.
I am an outstanding citizen.
Dealt a crushing blow that is life.
That is what life is.
One crushing blow after the next.
Some just take the blows better.
I am not that type.
I get hit and I fall deeper in my only despair.
Waiting for a lifeguard.
She was not at that bar
that night.
She was not my lifeguard.
When I sleep I will have dreams of that woman.
That was what I had.
A dream.
She will fill my head with hope.
I will wake with a smile.
I will then sink deep.
Deep
Realizing, she was the dream.

A dream girl not deserving my touch.
Some people fabricate with wood, metal, plastic
My fabrications are made of thoughts.
They are the strongest types.
They grip you.
Even fabricated into reality you would never attain this item.
She is this.
The unattainable.
I think I loved her.
How can you love a dream?
Something you never see or talk to.
Something.
Once in a life-
time
I sure hope someone finds this murderer.
This girl deserves justice.
Not in the way I deserve a perfect thing.
Silly of them to connect me.
I was alone having a drink that night.
Right now I'll have the same.
This time I have ice cube trays.
The girl on TV was lifeless.
The girl of my dreams had immense power.
She's still alive in my dreams, my head.
This girl is nothing like the girl I dream of.
I wonder.
This is such a stretch.
Some place, some bar.
Maybe I'll meet this dream girl.
We could have a chat.
Buy each other drinks.
Touch hands.
Intentional, but not seeming so.

We could then walk on the beach.
I think that would be wonderful.
I am such a fool to think of things.
Such things
they never happen
to a fool
like me.

About the Author

Kevin Mogged was born on June 4th, 1978 in the city of Shawano. He lived many years in Shawano before attending college in River Falls. He then lived near Lake Geneva and eventually circled back near his family in Shawano. He has many interests and hobbies. Kevin is very active in the local art scenes. Outside of writing, Kevin enjoys painting, sculpting, electronic music writing, SCUBA diving, traveling, photographing, computing, studying the natural world, and martial arts. Kevin enjoys various genres of music, books, and movies. His favorite genres are zombie and horror. He also enjoys motorcycling and bicycling.